POSSIBILITY
PURPOSE
ENDEAVOR

By the Same Compiler

1. FAITH, HOPE, LOVE
2. LOVE, FRIENDSHIP, GOOD CHEER
3. COURAGE, AMBITION, RESOLUTION
4. CONDUCT, HEALTH, GOOD FORTUNE
5. PATIENCE, PERSEVERANCE, ENDURANCE

Each 50 cents net

A. C. McCLURG & CO.
Publishers

POSSIBILITY
PURPOSE
ENDEAVOR

Compiled by
GRACE BROWNE STRAND

CHICAGO
A. C. McCLURG & CO.
1912

COPYRIGHT
A. C. McCLURG & CO.
1912

Published October, 1912

THE·PLIMPTON·PRESS
[W·D·O]
NORWOOD·MASS·U·S·A

POSSIBILITY

Our best thoughts come from others
                                Emerson

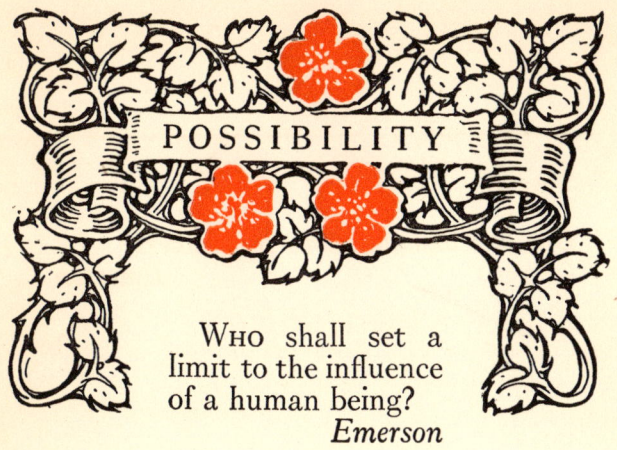

POSSIBILITY

Who shall set a limit to the influence of a human being?
Emerson

◆

The mind profits by the wreck of every passion, and we may measure our road to wisdom by the sorrows we have undergone. *Bulwer-Lytton*

◆

A word or a nod from the good has more weight than the eloquent speeches of others.
Plutarch

◆

I would that we might understand ourselves, see what we might be, our possibilities. *Phillips Brooks*

POSSIBILITY·PURPOSE·ENDEAVOR

Our deeds determine us as much as we determine our deeds. *George Eliot*

◆

He who lives in his thoughts, and the emotions which they awaken, needs little else for his entertainment; and as he needs little for himself he is the more able to be of help to others. *Bishop Spalding*

◆

If a man expects and believes great things of himself, it makes no odds where you put him. *Thoreau*

◆

For some there be, whose feet must fare,
  By common ways, who may not hear
Or, hearing, may not understand
  The linnet's song, so high and clear.

And I, who cannot tune my throat
  To pipe the linnet's golden lay,
May still, beside the common path,
  Sing mine own song in mine own way.
Florence Jones

POSSIBILITY · PURPOSE · ENDEAVOR

We mount to heaven mostly on the ruins of our cherished schemes, finding our failures were successes.
A. Bronson Alcott

◆

We are haunted by an ideal life, and it is because we have within us the beginning and the possibility of it.
Phillips Brooks

◆

Every heart that has beat strong and cheerful has left a hopeful impulse behind it in the world, and bettered the tradition of mankind. *Stevenson*

◆

Any Christian spirit working kindly in its little sphere, whatever it may be, will find its mortal life too short for its vast means of usefulness. *Charles Dickens*

◆

All things are possible to him that believeth. *St. Mark 9:23*

POSSIBILITY · PURPOSE · ENDEAVOR

There's a divinity that shapes our ends,
Rough-hew them how we will.
Shakespeare

❖

If we but will and work, opportunities are offered us to become and to perform whatever may crown and glorify a human soul.
Bishop Spalding

❖

The least moment is of importance to all nature. The entire ocean is affected by a pebble.
Pascal

❖

If anything is possible for man and conformable to his nature, think that this can be attained by thyself too.
Marcus Aurelius

❖

Let a man but have an aim, a purpose, and opportunities to attain his end shall start forth like buds at the kiss of spring.
Bishop Spalding

POSSIBILITY · PURPOSE · ENDEAVOR

We may be what we aspire to be.
Anon.

◆

A consideration of petty circumstances is the tomb of great things. *Voltaire*

◆

Nothing is useless to the man of sense; he turns everything to account.
La Fontaine

◆

'Tis in thy power to think as thou wilt.
Walter Pater

◆

Chiefly the mould of a man's fortune is in his own hands. *Bacon*

◆

Do not think that what is hard for thee to master is impossible for man; but if a thing is possible and proper to man, deem it attainable by thee.
Marcus Aurelius

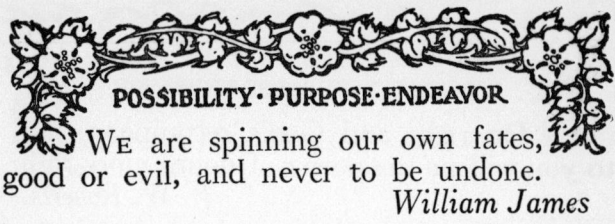

POSSIBILITY · PURPOSE · ENDEAVOR

WE are spinning our own fates, good or evil, and never to be undone.
William James

◆

EVERY day is a fresh beginning,
  Every morn is the world made new.
You who are weary of sorrow and sinning,
  Here is a beautiful hope for you;
A hope for me and a hope for you.
Susan Coolidge

◆

WHETHER any particular day shall bring you more of happiness or of suffering is largely beyond your power to determine. Whether each day of your life shall *give* happiness or suffering rests with yourself.
George S. Merriam

◆

IT is the secret sympathy,
The silver link, the silken tie,
Which heart to heart, and mind to mind
In body and in soul can bind.
Sir Walter Scott

POSSIBILITY · PURPOSE · ENDEAVOR

Do right and God's recompense to you will be the power of doing more right.
F. W. Roberts

◆

Look well into thyself; there is a source of strength which will always spring up if thou wilt always look there.
Marcus Aurelius

◆

Great things thro' greatest hazards are achiev'd,
And then they shine.
Beaumont and Fletcher

◆

Who goeth in the way that Christ has gone,
Is much more sure to meet with Him, than one
    That traveleth by-ways.
Perhaps my God, though He be far before,
May turn and take me by the hand, and more,
    May strengthen my decays.
George Herbert

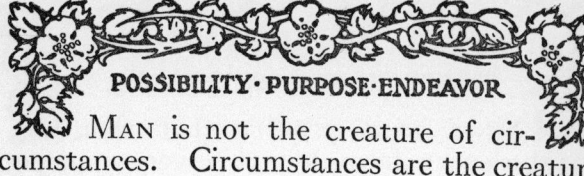

POSSIBILITY · PURPOSE · ENDEAVOR

Man is not the creature of circumstances. Circumstances are the creatures of man. *Disraeli*

◆

With God all things are possible.
Matthew 19: 26

◆

He who follows reason in all things is both tranquil and active at the same time, and also cheerful and collected. *Anon.*

◆

Human happiness, therefore, can only be complete as all the powers have their full and legitimate play. *Thomas*

◆

There is no field so small, no cranny so contracted, but that a great spirit can house and manifest itself therein. The thunder that smites the Alps into dust, can gather itself into the width of a golden wire.
Ruskin

POSSIBILITY · PURPOSE · ENDEAVOR

Since it is possible that thou mayst depart from life this very moment, regulate every act and thought accordingly.
Marcus Aurelius

◆

Nothing is impossible. There are ways which lead to everything.
La Rochefoucauld

◆

The wind that blows can never kill
    The tree God plants;
It bloweth east; it bloweth west;
The tender leaves have little rest,
But any wind that blows is best.
    The tree God plants
Strikes deeper root, grows higher still,
Spreads wider boughs, for God's good-will
    Meets all its wants.
Lillie E. Barr

◆

Do the truth ye know, and you shall learn the truth you need to know.
George Macdonald

POSSIBILITY · PURPOSE · ENDEAVOR

THE more you practice what you know, the more shall you know what to practice.   *W. Jenkins*

◆

MEN are often capable of greater things than they perform.   *Walpole*

◆

SEVEN hundred pounds and possibilities is good gifts.   *Shakespeare*

◆

I HAVE ever held it a maxim, never to do through another what it were possible for me to do myself.   *Montesquieu*

◆

AND what's impossible can't be,
And never never comes to pass.
   Colman

◆

GROWTH is the inevitable result of work done in the right direction.
   Waldo Pondray Warren

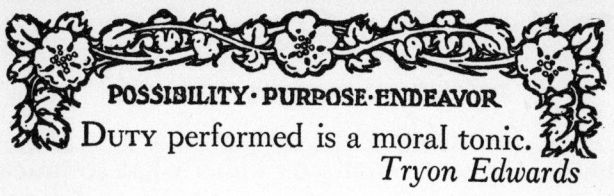

POSSIBILITY · PURPOSE · ENDEAVOR

Duty performed is a moral tonic.
Tryon Edwards

◆

There is no impossibility to him who stands prepared to conquer every hazard.
Sarah J. Hale

◆

Let us start up and live: here come moments that cannot be had again; some few may yet be filled with imperishable good.
J. Martineau

◆

To maintain oneself on this earth is not a hardship but a pastime, if only one will live simply and wisely. *Thoreau*

◆

Practice what you know, and it will help to make clear what now you do not know. *Rembrandt*

◆

Every duty which we omit obscures some truth which we should have known.
Ruskin

PURPOSE

PURPOSE

THE secret of success is constancy of purpose.
Disraeli

◆

IT is well to have visions of a better life than that of every day, but it is the life of every day from which elements of a better life must come. *Maurice Maeterlinck*

◆

IN doing is this knowledge won,
To see what yet remains undone.
With this our pride repress,
And give us grace, a growing store,
That day by day we may do more
And may esteem it less.
Bishop Trench

POSSIBILITY · PURPOSE · ENDEAVOR

WE are all of us made more graceful by the inward presence of what we believe to be a generous purpose. *George Eliot*

◆

HE that resolves upon any great and good end has, by that very resolution, scaled the chief barrier to it. *Tryon Edwards*

◆

WE are responsible, each in his own little way, for trying to leave this sad world happier. *Anon.*

◆

THEY who are most weary of life, and yet are most unwilling to die, are such who have lived to no purpose, who have rather breathed than lived. *Lord Clarendon*

◆

IF any man has any serious purpose in life, that which runs counter to it, or is foreign to it, will be looked at frowningly or carelessly by him. *Ruskin*

POSSIBILITY · PURPOSE · ENDEAVOR

LIFE is too short to waste
In critic peep or cynic bark,
Quarrel or reprimand:
'Twill soon be dark;
Up! mind thy own aim, and
God speed the mark.

Emerson

◆

HIGH aims and lofty purposes are the wings of the soul aiding it to mount to heaven.

S. Spring

◆

I WOULD be true, for there are those who trust me;
I would be pure, for there are those who care;
I would be strong, for there is much to suffer;
I would be brave, for there is much to dare;
I would be friend of all — the foe — the friendless;
I would be giving, and forget the gift;
I would be humble, for I know my weakness;
I would look up — and laugh — and love — and lift.

Howard Arnold Walter

POSSIBILITY · PURPOSE · ENDEAVOR

THE purpose of a journey is not only to arrive at the goal, but to find enjoyment on the way. *Henry Van Dyke*

◆

THIS world belongs to the energetic.
Emerson

◆

ALL life is a school, a preparation, a purpose. *Anon.*

◆

LIFE, in all ranks and situations, is an outward occupation, an actual and active work. *W. von Humboldt*

◆

GOD overrules all mutinous accidents, brings them under his laws of fate, and makes them all serviceable to his purpose.
Marcus Aurelius

◆

ALWAYS hold fast to your purpose, and you will win success. *Ruskin*

POSSIBILITY · PURPOSE · ENDEAVOR

If we have need of a strong will in order to do good, it is more necessary for us in order not to do evil. *Mole*

◆

I ask you while hope is still fresh and enthusiasm unchilled to gain some conception of the solemnity, the vastness, the unity, the purpose of life. *Bishop Westcott*

◆

Defer not till to-morrow to be wise;
To-morrow's sun to thee may never rise.
Congreve

◆

A purpose is the eternal condition of success. *T. T. Munger*

◆

All common things, each day's events,
That with the hour begin and end,
Our pleasures and our discontents,
Are rounds by which we may ascend.
Longfellow

POSSIBILITY · PURPOSE · ENDEAVOR

RESOLVE to perform what you ought; perform without fail what you resolve.
Benjamin Franklin

◆

HE who soweth bountifully shall reap also bountifully. God loveth a cheerful giver.
2 Cor. 9: 6, 7

◆

ONE good action, one temptation resisted and overcome, will prove a cordial for weak and low spirits far beyond that which either indulgence, or diversion, or company can do for them. *Anon.*

◆

Do nothing inconsiderately nor without a purpose. *Anon.*

◆

COMFORT me not! — for if ought be worse
 than failure from over-stress
Of a life's prime purpose, it is to sit down content with a little success.
Bulwer-Lytton

POSSIBILITY · PURPOSE · ENDEAVOR

It is part of a good man to do great and noble deeds though he risks everything in doing them. *Plutarch*

◆

What men want is not talent; it is purpose. *Bulwer-Lytton*

◆

I profess not talking: only this, let each man do his best. *Shakespeare*

◆

Every branch of knowledge which a good man possesses, he may apply to some good purpose. *C. Buchanan*

◆

Nothing is denied to well directed labor; nothing is ever to be attained without it.
Sir Joshua Reynolds

◆

Do not despise your situation; in it you must act, suffer, and conquer.
Anon.

POSSIBILITY · PURPOSE · ENDEAVOR

A MAN with a half-volition goes backwards and forwards, and makes no way on the smoothest road.
Anon.

◆

WORK to satisfy thine own nature, thine innermost craving for truth, beauty, and love, not to please another.
Bishop Spalding

◆

LEANING on Him, make with reverent meekness
    His own thy will,
And with strength from Him shall thy utter weakness
    Life's task fulfil.
Whittier

◆

TURN the full light on our lives, O Saviour Divine. Show us our deepest purposes. Make us honest with ourselves. Keep us pure in heart that we may always see Thee. Lead us to our own work.
Christian Reisner

POSSIBILITY · PURPOSE · ENDEAVOR

ONLY a great moral purpose can sustain a great soul, and a great moral purpose rests finally on faith in God.
Bishop Spalding

◆

EVERY noble activity makes room for itself. *Emerson*

◆

THE only failure a man ought to fear is failure in cleaving to the purpose he sees to be best. *George Eliot*

◆

THE flighty purpose never is o'ertook unless the deed go with it. *Shakespeare*

◆

MEN do less than they ought unless they do all that they can. *Carlyle*

◆

FIRMNESS of purpose is one of the most necessary sinews of character, and one of the best instruments of success.
Chesterfield

POSSIBILITY · PURPOSE · ENDEAVOR

It matters more which way one's face is set than how fast one proceeds.
Arthur Christopher Benson

◆

Character cannot be formed without action. *Arlo Bates*

◆

To live is sometimes very difficult, but it is never meritorious in itself; and we must have a reason to allege to our conscience why we shall continue to exist upon this crowded earth. *Stevenson*

◆

Everything exists for some end.
Marcus Aurelius

◆

Every purpose is established by counsel.
Proverbs 20: 18

◆

He who has a firm will molds the world to himself. *Goethe*

POSSIBILITY · PURPOSE · ENDEAVOR

Man is kept in life by work, and dies either because he will not, or because he cannot work. *Bates*

◆

A purpose once formed, and then death or victory, — this quality will do anything that is to be done in the world; and no talent, no circumstances, no opportunities, will make one a man without it. *Buxton*

◆

Abide in me; o'ershadow by Thy love
Each half-formed purpose and dark thought of sin;
Quench, ere it rise, each selfish, low desire,
And keep my soul as Thine, calm and divine.
H. B. Stowe

◆

He who lives to no purpose lives to a bad purpose.
W. Nevins

◆

Let no act be done without a purpose.
Marcus Aurelius

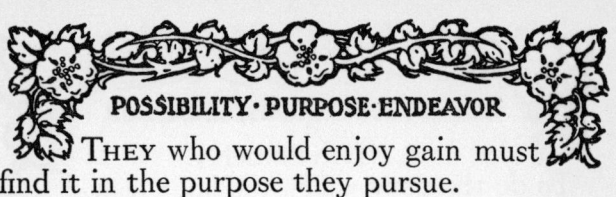

POSSIBILITY · PURPOSE · ENDEAVOR

They who would enjoy gain must find it in the purpose they pursue.
Mrs. Hale

◆

There is no action so slight, nor so mean, but it may be done to a great purpose and ennobled therefore; nor is any purpose so great that slight actions may not help it, and may be so done as to help it much, most especially that chief of all purposes, the pleasing of God.
Ruskin

◆

What to ourselves in passion we propose,
The passion ending, doth the purpose lose.
Shakespeare

◆

I would so live as if I knew that I received my being only for the benefit of others.
Seneca

◆

Our grand business is not to see what lies dimly at a distance, but to do what lies clearly at hand.
Carlyle

[32]

POSSIBILITY · PURPOSE · ENDEAVOR

Never delay
To do the duty which the hour brings,
Whether it be in great or smaller things;
For who doth know
What he shall do the coming day.

Anon.

◆

A man's greatness lies not in wealth and station, as the vulgar believe, nor yet in his intellectual capacity, which is often associated with the meanest moral character, the most abject servility to those in high places, and arrogance to the poor and lowly; but a man's true greatness lies in the consciousness of an honest purpose in life, founded on a just estimate of himself and everything else, on frequent self-examination, and a steady obedience to the rule which he knows to be right, without troubling himself about what others may think or say, or whether they do or do not do that which he thinks and says and does. *George Long*

◆

Act! the wise are known by their actions.
Salis

POSSIBILITY · PURPOSE · ENDEAVOR

Surely there is something to be done from morning till night and to find out what is the appointed work of the onward-tending soul.
Fanny Kemble

◆

To know what you prefer, instead of humbly saying Amen to what the world tells you you ought to prefer, is to have kept your soul alive. Such a man may be generous; he may be honest in something more than a commercial sense; he may love his friends with an elective, personal sympathy, and not accept them as an adjunct of the station to which he has been called. He may be a man, in short, acting on his own instincts, keeping in his own shape that God made him in; and not a mere crank in the social engine house, welded on principles that he does not understand, and for purposes that he does not care for.

Stevenson

◆

Let us satisfy our own consciences and trouble not ourselves by looking for fame.
Seneca

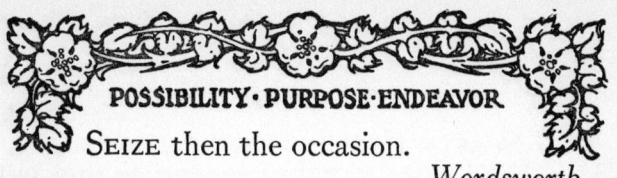

POSSIBILITY · PURPOSE · ENDEAVOR

Seize then the occasion.
Wordsworth

◆

Many good purposes and intentions lie in the churchyard. *Philip Henry*

◆

To everything there is a season, and a time to every purpose under the sun.
Ecclesiastes 3: 1

◆

It is aspiration that counts, not realization; pursuit, not achievement; quest, not conquest. *Beatrice Harraden*

◆

He who lives without a definite purpose achieves no higher end than to serve as a warning to others. *Anon.*

◆

I would not waste the springtime of my youth in idle dalliance; I would plant rich seeds to blossom in my manhood, and bear fruit when I am old. *Hillhouse*

POSSIBILITY · PURPOSE · ENDEAVOR

Man can only learn to rise by the consideration of that which he cannot surmount. *Richter*

◆

A good intention clothes itself with power. *Emerson*

◆

Have a purpose in life, and having it, throw into your work such strength of mind and muscle as God has given you. *Carlyle*

◆

A determinate purpose in life and a steady adhesion to it through all disadvantages, are indispensable conditions of success. *W. M. Punshon*

◆

Nothing is degrading which a high and noble purpose ennobles. *J. Martineau*

◆

Life is a short day; but it is a working day. *Hannah More*

POSSIBILITY · PURPOSE · ENDEAVOR

Do not, for one repulse, forego the purpose that you resolved to effect.
Shakespeare

◆

The strongest wind cannot stagger a Spirit; it is a Spirit's breath. A just man's purpose cannot be split on any Grampus or material rock, but itself will split rocks until it succeeds. *Thoreau*

◆

Thou camest not to thy place by accident,
It is the very place God meant for thee;
And shouldst thou there small scope for action see,
Do not for this give room for discontent.
Bishop Trench

◆

To secure a great end one must be willing to pay a great price. *Anon.*

◆

Do thy duty while it is in your power to choose. *William Smith*

POSSIBILITY · PURPOSE · ENDEAVOR

If we are quite sure that that which we propose or have done is best, then we may with easy conscience stand by our colors. *J. M. Stifler*

◆

Let me but do my work from day to day
   In field or forest, at the desk or loom,
   In roaring market place or tranquil room;
Let me but find it in my heart to say,
When vagrant wishes beckon me astray,
   "This is my work; my blessing, not my doom.
   Of all who live, I am the one by whom
This work can best be done in the right way."
Henry Van Dyke

◆

It is wonderful what strength of purpose will come from the feeling that we are in the way of duty. *Fanny Edwards*

◆

Whether a life is noble or ignoble depends not on the calling which is adopted, but on the spirit in which it is followed. *Anon.*

ENDEAVOR

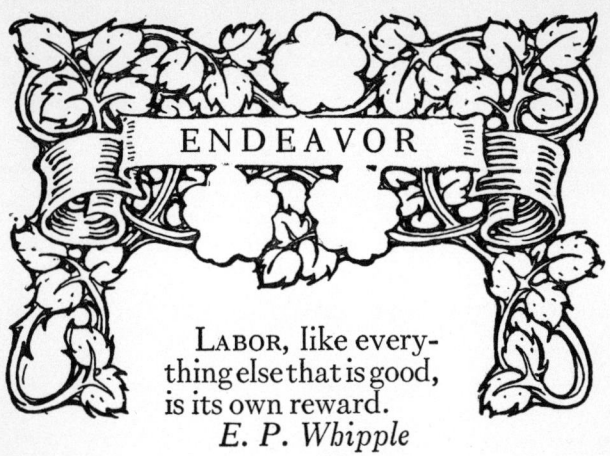

ENDEAVOR

L̲ABOR̲, like everything else that is good, is its own reward.
E. P. Whipple

◆

S̲OME̲ place the bliss in action, some in ease, Those call it pleasure, and contentment, these. *Pope*

◆

T̲HY̲ actions, and thy actions alone, determine thy worth. *Fichte*

◆

I̲F̲ a man constantly aspires, is he not elevated? Did ever a man try heroism, magnanimity, truth, sincerity, and find that there was no advantage in them? That it was a vain endeavor? *Thoreau*

POSSIBILITY · PURPOSE · ENDEAVOR

Doing is the great thing.
Ruskin

◆

The fire-fly only shines when on the wing; so it is with the mind; when we rest we darken.
Bailey

◆

If we are not here to try to do the best, in my humble opinion, the sooner we are away the better for all parties.
Stevenson

◆

What is difficulty? Only a word indicating the degree of strength requisite for accomplishing particular objects; a mere notice of the necessity for exertion.
Anon.

◆

There is a tide in the affairs of men,
Which, taken at the flood, leads on to fortune;
Omitted, all the voyage of their life
Is bound in shallows, and in miseries.
Shakespeare

POSSIBILITY · PURPOSE · ENDEAVOR

The true worth of a man is to be measured by the objects he pursues.
Marcus Aurelius

◆

Our worth is determined by the good deeds we do, rather than by the fine emotions we feel. *E. L. Magoon*

◆

He who prays as he ought, will endeavor to live as he prays. *Owen*

◆

'Tis not what man does which exalts him, but what man would do. *Browning*

◆

The man who seeks one, and but one, thing in life may hope to achieve it.
Bulwer-Lytton

◆

It is not for man to rest in absolute contentment. He is born to hopes and aspirations. - *Southey*

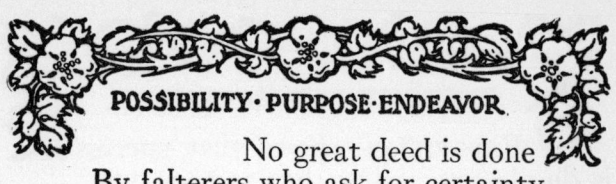

POSSIBILITY · PURPOSE · ENDEAVOR

No great deed is done
By falterers who ask for certainty.
George Eliot

◆

WHAT man knows should find expression in what he does. *Bovee*

◆

WE must be doing something to be happy. *Hazlitt*

◆

IN great attempts it is glorious even to fail. *Longinus*

◆

THINGS out of hope are compass'd oft with venturing. *Shakespeare*

◆

THE fact is, to do anything in this world worth doing, we must not stand back shivering and thinking of the cold and danger, but jump in and scramble through as well as we can. *Sidney Smith*

POSSIBILITY · PURPOSE · ENDEAVOR

EXPERIENCE shows that success is due less to ability than to endeavor.
Anon.

◆

IT is a very great thing for us to do the very best we can do, just where and as we are. *Babcock*

◆

MAKE your failure tragical by the earnestness of your endeavor, and then it will not differ from success. *Thoreau*

◆

BE sure no man was ever discontented with the world who did his duty in it.
Southey

◆

IF you would create something, you must be something. *Goethe*

◆

ORDER thy life well in every single act.
Marcus Aurelius

POSSIBILITY · PURPOSE · ENDEAVOR

May I reach
That purest heaven, be to other souls
The cup of strength in some great agony,
Enkindle generous ardor, feed pure love,
Be the sweet presence of a good diffused,
And in diffusion ever more intense!
So shall I join the choir invisible
Whose music is the gladness of the world.

George Eliot

◆

It is the over curious ambition of many to be best, or to be none. If they may not do so well as they would, they will not do as well as they may. I will do my best to do my best, and what I want in power, supply in will. Thus whilst I pay in part, I shall not be a debtor for all. He owes most who pays nothing.

Arthur Warwick

◆

We want an aim that can never grow vile, and then never lay aside our endeavor. In this way only can we have happiness and success. *Anon.*

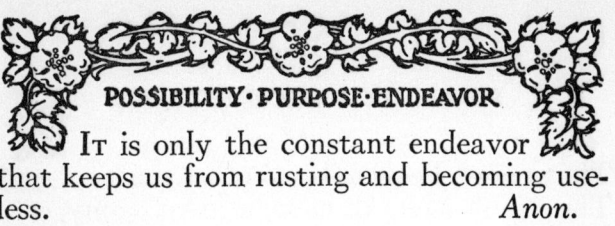

POSSIBILITY · PURPOSE · ENDEAVOR

It is only the constant endeavor that keeps us from rusting and becoming useless.
Anon.

◆

How strangely high endeavor may be blessed,
Where piety and valor jointly go.
Dryden

◆

If you don't do better to-day you'll do worse to-morrow.
Anon.

◆

Good thoughts, though God accept them, yet toward men are little better than good dreams, except they be put into action.
Bacon

◆

The best things are nearest: light in your eyes, flowers at your feet, duties at your hand, the path of God just before you. Then do not grasp at the stars, but endeavor to do life's common work as it comes.
Anon.

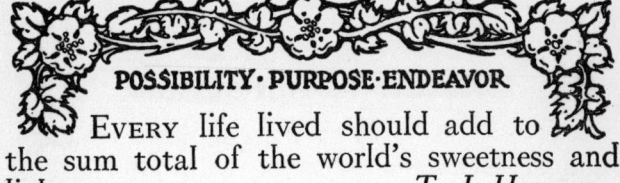

POSSIBILITY · PURPOSE · ENDEAVOR

Every life lived should add to the sum total of the world's sweetness and light. *T. J. Hosmer*

◆

Help thyself, and God will help thee.
George Herbert

◆

As we must ask of God whatsoever we need, so we must watch and labor for all that we ask. *Jeremy Taylor*

◆

Dream manfully and nobly, and thy dreams shall be prophets, but thou must also endeavor. *Anon.*

◆

In our doing; and our best doing is our best enjoyment. *Jacobi*

◆

The movement of the species is upward, irresistibly upward. *Bancroft*

POSSIBILITY · PURPOSE · ENDEAVOR

Yet I argue not
Against Heaven's hand or will, nor bate a jot
Of heart or hope; but still bear up and steer
Right onward.

Milton

◆

We would never stir a finger, if only on condition of being guaranteed against oversights, misinformation, mistakes, ignorance, loss, and danger. *H. Martineau*

◆

So nigh is grandeur to our dust,
 So near is God to man,
When duty whispers low, Thou must,
 The youth replies, I can.

Emerson

◆

What we truly and earnestly aspire to be, that in some sense we are.

Mrs. Jameson

POSSIBILITY · PURPOSE · ENDEAVOR

Find out your work and stand to it; the night cometh when no man can work.
Carlyle

❖

High aims form high character, and great objects bring out great minds.
John A. Andrews

❖

The practices of good men are more subject to error than their speculations. I will, then, honor good examples, but endeavor to live according to good precepts.
Bishop Hall

❖

Endeavor to attend to the matter before thee with all the strength that God has given you.
J. A. Burnes

❖

Aim at the sun, and you may not reach it; but your arrow will fly far higher than if aimed at an object on a level with yourself.
J. Hawes

POSSIBILITY · PURPOSE · ENDEAVOR

OH, there is no man, no woman, so small that they cannot make their life great by high endeavor.
Carlyle

◆

NOT failure but low aim is crime.
Lowell

◆

RISE . . . as children learn, be thou
Wiser for falling.
Tennyson

◆

BE always doing something serviceable to mankind.
Marcus Aurelius

◆

THE real merit is not in the success, but in the endeavor.
W. M. Punshon

◆

CATCH, then, O catch, the transient hour;
  Improve each moment as it flies;
Life's a short summer — man a flower —
  He dies — alas! how soon he dies.
Samuel Johnson

POSSIBILITY · PURPOSE · ENDEAVOR

ENDEAVOR may not always bring happiness, but there is no happiness without endeavor.
Disraeli

◆

THIS court of the past differs from all living aristocracy in this: it is open to labor and to merit, but to nothing else. No wealth will bribe, no name overawe, no artifice deceive, the guardian of these Elysian gates. . . . Do you deserve to enter? Pass. Do you ask to be the companions of nobles? Make yourself noble and you shall be.
Ruskin

◆

SET your shoulder joyously to the world's wheel. *Havelock Ellis*

◆

SPEND yourself on the work before you.
Emerson

◆

THERE never was a right endeavor but it succeeded. *Emerson*

POSSIBILITY · PURPOSE · ENDEAVOR

EVEN if I faint by the roadside
... it is something to be on the road that
leads to the High Ideals. *Anon.*

◆

LIFE was not given for indolent contemplation and study of self. Actions, and actions only, determine thy worth. *Fichte*

◆

THE fruit that can fall without shaking,
Indeed is too mellow for me.
   Lady Montague

◆

How can we live and think that any one
has trouble — piercing trouble — and we
could help them and never try.
   George Eliot

◆

IF you want knowledge, you must toil
for it; if food, you must toil for it; and if
pleasure, you must toil for it. *Ruskin*

POSSIBILITY · PURPOSE · ENDEAVOR

ONE who desires to excel should endeavor to do it in those things which are in themselves most excellent. *Epictetus*

◆

HE is wise who finds a teacher in every man, an occasion to improve in every happening, for whom nothing is useless or in vain. *Bishop Spalding*

◆

IT is the struggle toward an ideal, the constant effort to get higher and further which develops manhood and character.
E. Rexford

◆

OH, dream no more of quiet life,
Care finds the careless out; more wise to vow
   Thy heart entire to faith's pure strife;
So peace will come, thou knowest not when or how.

Lyra Apostolica

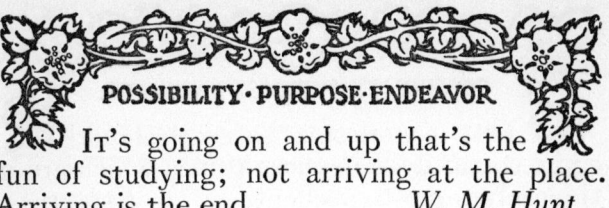
POSSIBILITY · PURPOSE · ENDEAVOR

It's going on and up that's the fun of studying; not arriving at the place. Arriving is the end. *W. M. Hunt*

◆

The more we do the more we can do.
Hazlitt

◆

In idleness alone is there perpetual despair. *Carlyle*

◆

Fame is the spur that the clear spirit doth raise,
That last infirmity of noble minds,
To scorn delights and live laborious days:
But the fair guerdon when we hope to find,
And think to burst out into sudden blaze,
Comes the blind Fury with th' abhorred shears,
And slits the thin-spun life, "But not the praise,"
Phœbus replied, and touched my trembling ears. *Milton*

[55]

POSSIBILITY · PURPOSE · ENDEAVOR

The thoroughly great men are those who have done everything thoroughly, and who have never despised anything, however small, of God's making. *Ruskin*

◆

If I were you, I would not worry. Just make up your mind to do better when you get another chance. *Beatrice Harraden*

◆

To travel hopefully is better than to arrive, and the true success is to labor.

Stevenson

◆

Constant activity in doing good, and endeavoring to make others happy is one of the surest ways of making ourselves so.

Anon.

◆

All things come to him who waits — and labors while he waits.

Robert A. Campbell

POSSIBILITY · PURPOSE · ENDEAVOR

Be thy aim not increase of happiness, but of knowledge, wisdom, power, and virtue; and thou shalt, without thinking of it, find thyself happy. *Bishop Spalding*

◆

Build thee more stately mansions, O my soul,
As the swift seasons roll!
Leave thy low-vaulted past!
Let each new temple, nobler than the last,
Shut thee from heaven with a dome more vast,
Till thou at length art free,
Leaving thine outgrown shell by life's unresting sea!
Holmes

◆

Our duty is to be useful, not according to our desires, but according to our powers.
Anon.

◆

Heaven never helps the man who will not act. *Sophocles*

POSSIBILITY · PURPOSE · ENDEAVOR

Aim at perfection in everything.
Chesterfield

◆

Let a man contend to the uttermost
For his life's set prize, be it what it will.
Browning

◆

The only man who never makes a mistake is the man who never does anything.
Theodore Roosevelt

◆

"What helped you over the great obstacles of life?" was asked a man. "The other obstacles," he replied. *Anon.*

◆

To live is not merely to breathe, it is to act. *Rousseau*

◆

The wise and active conquer difficulties by daring to attempt them. *Rowe*

POSSIBILITY · PURPOSE · ENDEAVOR

I HAVE lived to know that the secret of happiness is never to allow your energies to stagnate. *Adams Clarke*

◆

THE end of man is action and not thought, though it be of the noblest. *Carlyle*

The End